A Guide to
THE ICONS
OF THE
LAKE DISTRICT

by
David Watson

First published in 2009 by
Photoprint Scotland

© David & Rosemary Watson
 watson.dr@btinternet.com

ISBN 978-0-9559438-5-0

Photographs by David & Rosemary Watson
Additional photography see page 84
Graphics and design by Rosemary Watson

Printed and bound by MLG, Glasgow

CONTENTS

About the maps

Where sketch maps are used, they are Simple Maps giving only essential information to navigate to iconic features. For more detail, consult OS Landranger maps 89,90, 96 and 97.

INTRODUCTION

Close your eyes and think of England. What do you see? Big Ben, the Queen, Stonehenge? These are the "icons", the essential images, which epitomise the country.

The renowned Kendal Mint Cake

John Peel

This book identifies over 40 "Icons". Each one is illustrated with at least one photograph, and where there is a potential visit, there is a "How to get there" box, and inclusion on a Simple Map. There are grid references and contact information, including phone numbers and web sites.

Over the 200 or so years of tourism , iconic people, places, events and traditions for the Lake District have also become embedded in the public mind. They include people such as Words-worth and John Peel, places like Friar's Crag and the Bowder Stone, events such as Grasmere Sports and activities like cruising the lakes.

The Bowder Stone

The choice of the icons included is inevitably personal. Generally, mountains and fells are not included, as these are well covered in the wealth of other literature.

End of the cruise at Lakeside, Windermere

THROUGHOUT THE LAKE DISTRICT

The icons found throughout the Lake District tend to be products of centuries of tradition, often representing the influence of waves of settlers such as the Vikings. Only a few like the National Trust or the National Park are relatively recent.

Start of a hound trail near Lazonby

WARNING Standing up will affect the stability of the boat

Keswick Landings

STEAMBOATS AND LAKE CRUISES

If you are not visiting the Lake District to walk or to climb, the one most likely thing you will do is to take a cruise on one of the four lakes with scheduled services. Reportedly the most popular single activity for visitors to the Lake District is a cruise on Windermere. Commercial steamboats began in the Lake District during the mid-19th century, and although the only steam-powered boat remaining is on Lake Coniston, several of the original boats remain, but are powered now by diesel engines.

There are scheduled passenger services on four lakes, Windermere, Ullswater, Derwentwater and Coniston. Details of locations and contacts are contained in the sections dealing with North Lakes and South Lakes.

There is something truly idyllic about a lake cruise, especially after the hustle and bustle of the journey to get to the Lake District. There are lots of possibilities, ranging from the small-scale traditional launches used on Derwentwater, to vessels taking over 500 passengers on Windermere. Some of the boats are truly elegant, including especially those on Ullswater and the National Trust-owned Gondola, the only scheduled steamboat, on Coniston. You can combine your cruise with a range of options, with many "sail there" and "walk back" possibilities. On Windermere you can combine your cruise with a trip of the steam-powered Lakeside to Haverthwaite railway.

At Windermere you will also find the Windermere Steamboat Museum, which maintains a collection of historic steamboats dating back to the 1850s.

Early morning at Boness

For further details, see pages 50-51, for Derwentwater, 54-55 for Ullswater, 62-63 for Coniston and 74-75 for Windermere.

For Windermere Steamboat Museum, contact: 01539 445 565
www.steamboat.co.uk
steamboat@ecosse.net

Dash Beck, North of Skiddaw

Yew Tree Farm, Borrowdale

West approach to Hardnott

Kentmere Valley

Limestones south of Kendal

8

DRY STONE WALLS

Dry Stone Walls are built free from mortar or cement, and although they are found throughout Britain wherever there is available stone, they form an iconic part of the landscape of the Lake District.

Some walls are very old, but most date from the enclosure movement starting after the medieval period. Many of Lakeland's upland stone walls were sanctioned by Act of Parliament during the enclosures of the 18th and 19th centuries, especially the Enclosures Act of 1801.

The Lake District was ideal for the building of dry stone walls because of the general availability of stone, left scattered across the landscape by the retreating ice.

Stone walls often provide fascinating evidence of both the underlying geology and also the effect of the main rock transporter, glaciation.

The northern lakes area is dominated by the so-called Skiddaw Slate, an assortment of ancient slates, shales and mudstones. Sometimes the rock is well-bedded providing the flat stones which make wall-building much easier. The area to the south, with its Silurian slates is similar, and the walls may be neat and regular, but not always.

In the central fells, the Borrowdale Volcanic rocks make for a more rugged and varied style of stone walling. Around the edges of the Lake District, a ring of Carboniferous Limestone produces the regular silver grey walls south of Kendal and in the Shap area. In the west the igneous rocks of the central Lake District give way to sandstones, best seen at St Bees, where the walls are made of red-brown regular shaped blocks.

Demonstration wall at Ruskin Museum

An excellent place to see dry stone walling of various types is at the Ruskin Museum at Coniston. Here dry-stone waller Andrew Loudon has created different walls illustrating the use of different stone and techniques. The museum website gives an interesting insight into dry stone wall building. www.ruskinmuseum.com

How to get there
The Ruskin Museum is located in Coniston Village at the northern end of Coniston Water, just off the A593. It is accessible from the A591 (Ambleside) or from the M6 and South Lakes road, the A590(T).

For the whole selection of fell-running
records see www.bobgrahamclub.org.uk
To check out the range of fell running
events held annually throughout UK, see
www.fellrunner.org.uk

FELL RACING
THE BOB GRAHAM ROUND

Along with Hound Trails and Cumberland and Westmorland wrestling, fell racing probably began in the Lake District. It is still found in annual Lakeland sports events today.

The term fell racing covers a wide range of possibilities, from a 12 minute lung-bursting dash up Butter crag on Grasmere Sports Day, to the 27,000 feet of ascent of the Bob Graham Round. The sport is now well established wherever there are hills to run up, but its home was indisputably the Lake District. The website "Fell Running" has a lovely description of the sport, "the ultimate in adventurous independence, running free as the wind over the high peaks and ridges, mountain rocks and streams".

Fell racing probably began as a series of informal contests between farm labourers and shepherds. It developed into a formalised sport in the 1800s, and the first Grasmere "guides" race was held in 1869. The present long distance fell races started in the 20th century, with one tradition being established by the famous Bob Graham in the 1930s.

In 1932 Bob Graham, a Keswick guest-house owner traversed 42 fells, including all the 3000 foot peaks, in 24 hours. In doing so, he covered about 65 miles (104km) and ascended about 27,000 feet (8200m). It took 28 years before the feat was bettered.

Starting and finishing at the Moot Hall in Keswick, the 42-top traverse became known as the Bob Graham Round, and those who achieve it in 24 hours become eligible for the Bob Graham Club. Over the past 50 years the record has now been bettered many times and presently stands to Billy Bland (1982), with an amazing time of 13 hours and 53 minutes. The fastest woman is Ann Stentiford (1991) with 18 hours and 49 minutes.

During the last 50 years a host of different records have been set as fell runners sought out more and more challenges, In 1997 Mark Hartell achieved 77 peaks in 23 hours and 47 minutes, and in 2005 Yiannis Tridimas completed 60 peaks at the age of 60.

HERDWICKS

The name "Herdwick" refers to the almost wild sheep which roam the fells of the Lake District and contribute so much to the nature of the landscape. "Herdwick" most likely originated from the Old English word *heordewic*, and meant "sheep farm" as opposed to an "arable" or "crop farm". In Cumbria a "herdwick" initially described the piece of land under the control of each shepherd. Today it is the name of the breed of sheep, possibly originating in Norway.

Herdwick sheep have a number of qualities which combine to make them unique.

Almost like wild animal species which are territorial rather than migratory, Herdwick sheep stay on their own traditional area, not straying over into an adjacent valley, even in unfenced land. The local expression is that they are "heafed to the fell".

They are much more naturally resistant to disease and parasites than most other, softer breeds, and since they are incredibly hardy, they stay on the fells in all weathers, even in deep snow. It is to the farming of Herdwicks that we owe responsibility for the creation and continuation of the idyllic Lakeland habitat. Many people have the idea that the landscape is "natural", but in fact it is the product of hundreds of years of Herdwick sheep grazing and management.

If only simple economics prevailed, Herdwick sheep would have already disappeared from the fells. They are small, have only one lamb and their wool has little value. However, thanks to a combination of the National Trust and the acceptance by successive governments of the part Herdwicks play in the conservation of this invaluable national treasure, farming of the breed will likely continue into the future.

The famous writer of children's stories, Beatrix Potter, though starting life in London, became an expert breeder and judge of Herdwicks. When she died and left all her 14 farms and 4000 acres of land to the National Trust in 1943, she stipulated that only pure-bred Herdwicks should be farmed.

Many Herdwick lambs are black

Mature Herdwicks vary in colour

Trail hounds crossing Shap Beck

HOUND TRAILING

Of all the cultural activities associated with the Lake District, hound trailing is one of the most unique. A hound trail is a race, over the fells or through farmland, where specially bred dogs, similar to fox hounds, follow a scent trail of aniseed and paraffin, which has been laid down for the race. Races occur during the summer months and cover up to 8 miles.

The start of a hound trail near Lazonby

Most of us in UK are familiar with the traditional image of fox hounds. Trail hounds are similar, but lighter, leaner and faster, having been bred for the purpose of racing over many generations. Most races in the Lake District are held under the control of the Hound Trailing Association, first established in 1906, or the Border Hound Trailing Association, established in 1933, which looks after the interests of the many trail enthusiasts in north Cumbria and the borders. The season starts at the beginning of March and runs through to the end of October, with four or five events for different classes at each meeting.

The hound trailing fraternity is a very tight-knit group of enthusiasts, much like horse racing, where the sport has been part of the family for generations. To many it has become a way of life. Many hound trails take place in conjunction with other events such as agricultural shows and sports days. Before the races, a sack dipped in a mixture of paraffin and aniseed is dragged around the circular course. Usually there are four events, "puppies", "maidens", "seniors" and "veterans". A great deal of betting takes place so the trails are always well attended by bookmakers.

The finish of each race is always exciting and a tradition has grown up over the years of the owners at the finish blowing whistles, screaming and shouting as their hounds appear for the final run in.

Both hound trail associations have a strong tradition of support for local charities, ranging from the local village hall to Cumbria Air Ambulance.

www.houndtrailing.org.uk
www.borderhoundtrailing.com

Hounds in full flight in Borrowdale

How to join the National Trust

The easiest way is to join on line, where you will find a variety of membership packages, ranging from children to individual adults and families. In general it is beneficial to pay annual subscriptions by direct debit.

See www.nationaltrust.org

This is what the website tells us about membership benefits.

Join the National Trust today and youll enjoy:

* FREE entry and parking at more than 300 historic houses and gardens.
* FREE parking at our countryside and coastline locations.
* Members' Handbook – the complete guide to all of the places you can visit.
* Regional Newsletters packed with details of special events at locations near you.
* Three editions of our magazine, featuring news, views, gardening and letters, exclusively for members.
* Information about Centres and Associations in your area.

THE NATIONAL TRUST

The National Trust is probably the second most important institution in the Lake District after the National Park Authority, and it is certainly the biggest landowner. So what is the National Trust and what does it do?

The core purpose of the National Trust was defined in the National Trust Act of 1907, and remains so today.

"The National Trust shall be established for the purpose of promoting the permanent preservation for the benefit of the nation of lands and tenements (including buildings) of beauty or historic interest and as regards lands for the preservation (so far as is practicable) of their natural aspect, features and animal and plant life."

In other words the National Trust was set up, as a charity, to be the guardian of what we now call our "natural heritage" in all its forms.

Although the National Trust Act of Parliament dates from 1907, the Trust was actually founded in 1895 by three like-minded philanthropists, Octavia Hill, Hardwicke Rawnsley and Robert Hunter, who all saw the countryside under great threat from the developments of the Industrial Revolution.

Today the National Trust is guardian of over 240,000 hectares of our most beautiful land, over 700 miles of coastline and 200 historic buildings.

In the Lake District the National Trust is guardian of over a quarter of the land in the National Park, including many of the iconic landscapes and locations we mention in this book. Ninety farms are owned by the Trust, maintaining the traditional style of farming so vital for the preservation of the Lake District's unique landscape. Beatrix Potter was an early benefactor, leaving 4,000 acres to the Trust on her death.

National Trust properties are clearly shown on Ordnance Survey maps, which differentiate between those properties always open to the public and those with restricted access of some sort.

Yew Tree Farm, Coniston - left to the National Trust by Beatrix Potter

Lake District
National Park
Visitor Centre

OPEN

Daily 10am - 5pm
Free entry • Pay and display car park

The Purposes of the National Park
"The Lake District National Park Authority is a local government body which has the following purposes:
• To conserve and enhance the natural beauty, wildlife and cultural heritage of the Lake District.
• To promote opportunities for the understanding and enjoyment of the special qualities of the National Park.
• To seek to foster the economic and social well-being of local communities within the park."
The most powerful tool that the park authority has to achieve these purposes is through being the National Park planning authority.

THE LAKE DISTRICT NATIONAL PARK

If you are reading this in the Lake District, you are in the National Park. But you didn't pass through an entrance gate or pay a fee to enter the park. The reason is that the concept of national parks in UK is very different from that in USA, Australia or the Serengeti of Tanzania.

Britain's national parks have no gates, and they remain home to hundreds of farmers and thousands of people who live in the towns and villages within the park. The land remains owned by individuals or by the National Trust and the Forestry Commission.

The Lake District National Park is England's biggest national park at 2292 sq km (880 sq miles). It was established in 1951 and its official purpose goes a long way to explain its influence on the Lake District.

So, as well as being this incredible area of natural beauty the Lake District National Park is also home to over 42,000 people. There are hundreds of farms, scores of villages and three large settlements, Windermere, Keswick and Ambleside.

There are many unique cultural and social aspects to the park, and without the protection of the National Park planning controls, together with the input of bodies like the National Trust, many of the treasured and preserved ways of life would have long-since disappeared, especially the apparently inefficient and uneconomic Lakeland farming. But the National Park recognises the importance both of cultural heritage and also the essential contributions of different activities, but especially farming, to the unique Lake District landscape.

You will notice the lack of intrusive new housing developments, and the continuing use of local stone in buildings. In many ways the cultural landscape remains in harmony with the physical landscape and the rocks.

The Lake District National Park has over 12 million visitors per year, the vast majority of whom come by car, especially via the M6 motorway. About a third of employment in the park depends directly on tourism.

"Simple Map" showing Brockhole National Park Visitor Centre

www.lake-district.gov.uk

SIMPLE GUIDES

PLACE NAMES
OF THE LAKE DISTRICT

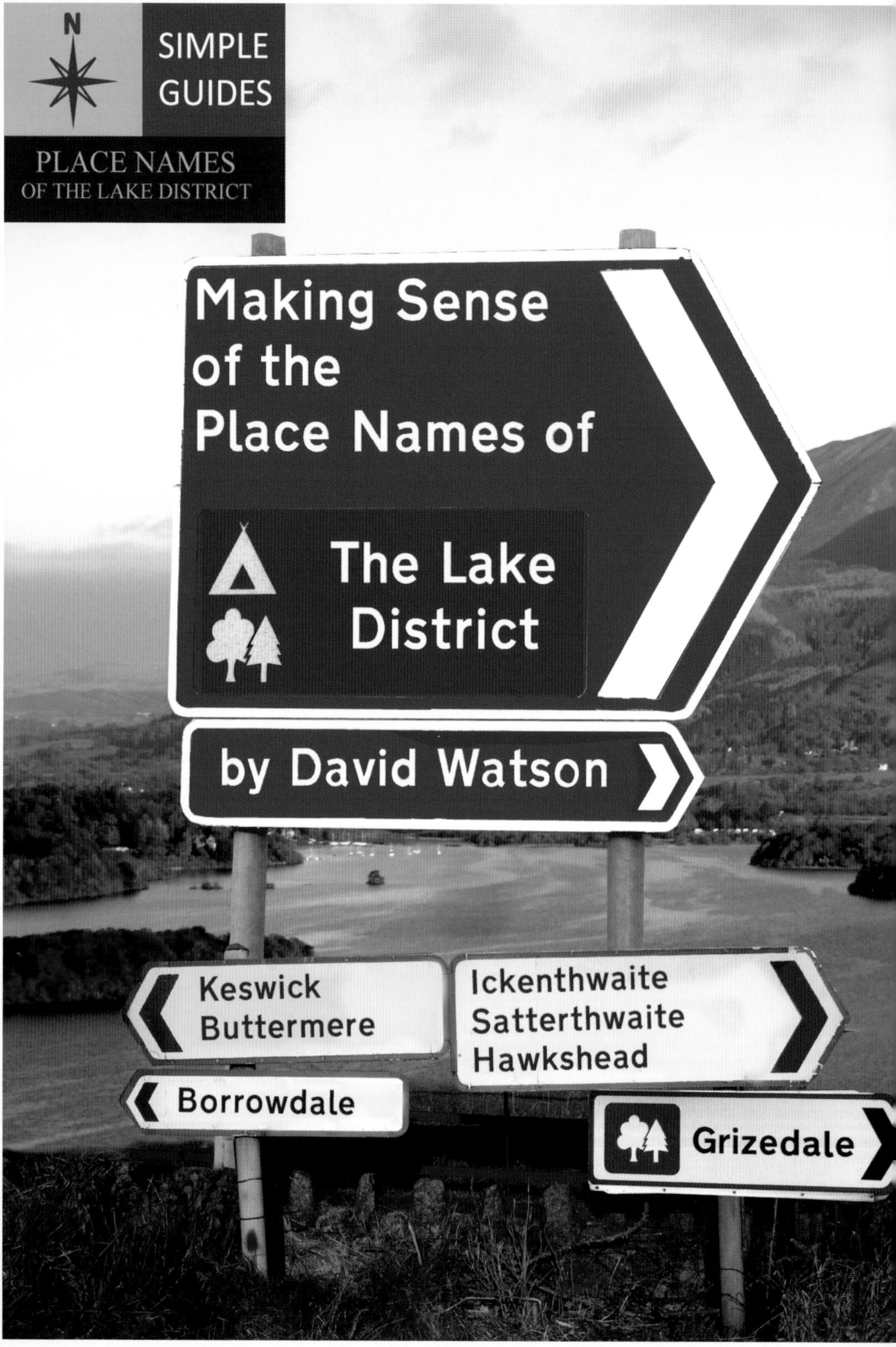

Making Sense of the Place Names of
The Lake District
by David Watson
Keswick
Buttermere
Borrowdale
Ickenthwaite
Satterthwaite
Hawkshead
Grizedale

YAN, TAN, TETHERA

"Yan, Tan, Tethera" or "One, Two, Three". The remnant of the ancient Cumbric language, still used on Lake District hill farms during living memory. One only has to look at the place names of the Lake District to see the influence of different linguistic groups as they settled the area over the last two thousand years.

The oldest names are generally those of the rivers, and their origins are usually lost in time. When the Romans arrived in the 1st century AD, they found a people speaking Cumbric, a version of Brythonic Celtic, the language which remains in Wales, Cornwall and Brittany today. Most has gone from Cumbria, but the numbers, "yan, tan tethera" used by shepherds for counting sheep,remained in use well into the 20th century. A few place names are traceable back to Cumbric. "Blencathra", meaning a "chair shaped mountain" is a good example.

By far the most iconic Lakeland names are those left by the settlers who originated in western Norway, and who came to Cumbria in the 9th century via the Isle of Man, Ireland and Scotland. They spoke the language we now refer to as "Old Norse" and were responsible for many of the names we still find throughout the Lake District. Amongst them are "beck", meaning a "stream", "fell" referring to a "mountain" and the most common place name of all "thwaite", meaning a "clearing". Although some names were gradually anglicised and others influenced by the Norman Conquest, many of the old place names remained, or became hybrids, with elements of Old Norse together with those of other languages, perhaps Middle English and occasionally French.

The result today is a mosaic of names of towns, villages, rivers, lakes and mountains, all of which have a meaning, and which bear testimony to the rich cultural and linguistic heritage which makes the Lake District so unique.

To find out more

For a simple guide to the meanings of Lake District place names, refer to the author's "Making Sense of the Place Names of the Lake District" where you will find the derivations and meanings of about 500 place names explained in fairly simple language.

If you wish to get really into the subject, check out "A Dictionary of Lake District Place Names" by Diana Whaley.

A selection of Cumbrian place names

CUMBERLAND SAUSAGE

Cumberland Sausages are a traditional sausage quite unlike any other in the UK, originating in Cumberland, the county which preceded the present Cumbria.

The sausages are quite distinctive. They are usually in a long, coiled roll, as opposed to the normal short "links". The sausages are usually thicker than the norm, and the texture is coarser. Traditionally the pork meat they contain is chopped rather than minced, and if it is "minced" the mincing machine should have a much coarser setting than for most sausages. There should be a minimum of 80% meat content.

Often the sausages are more highly seasoned than most, reflecting the availability of spices through the historic port of Whitehaven. Normally the sausages have lots of pepper in them. Traditionally there is no added colouring or preservative.

Above all, Cumberland Sausage is delicious and is normally served in a very simple way, as "Cumberland Sausage and Mash", often with onions or "onion gravy". If the sausage is cooked in its original coil, it may be easiest to do it in a medium oven rather than frying or grilling.

The Cumberland Sausage Association was set up in 2005 to protect the geographical status of Cumberland Sausage, much in the same way as Melton Mawbray Pies, Parma Ham or Champagne. Members agree to a set of minimum standards and are in the process of applying to the European Union for Protected Geographical Indicator status. Apart from the method of production, Cumberland Sausages must be made in Cumbria. Presently the Association has over 20 producers.

Cumberland Sausage Association
Telephone: 01539 732736
www.traditionalcumberlandsausage.com

A Cumberland Sausage Recipe
The author enjoys a casserole with Cumberland Sausage, chopped bacon or ham, mushrooms, red wine, shallots, garlic, bay leaf and thyme, all well-seasoned, cooked for an hour, thickened with a little plain flour and served with traditional vegetables.

Oven-cooked Cumberland sausage

WRESTLING, CUMBERLAND AND WESTMORLAND STYLE

Peninsulas develop and retain their own culture because of their relative isolation. We see it in Cornwall, Wales, Scotland, and in Cumbria. The origins of the peculiar style of Cumberland and Westmorland Wrestling are unknown. Some claim it to have a Norse origin, whereas others suggest a much older Celtic connection, with similarities to traditions in Cornwall and in Brittany. Wrestling takes place at open-air events such as Grasmere Sports and is quite different from what one normally thinks of as "wrestling". Competitors are attired in often richly embroidered vests, coloured briefs, and what can only be described as white "long johns". Wrestlers also always wear socks.

Traditionally over the last few centuries, wrestlers have come mainly from two sources, either from the farming communities or from mining. Today, with deep mining of both coal and iron ore more or less finished, most Cumberland and Westmorland wrestlers come from young farmers clubs. Both the Northern and Southern Federations of Young Farmers' Clubs include wrestling as an important part of their field days. There are wrestling academies at both Carlisle and Kendal.
 As well as sporting events, wrestling also occurs at agricultural shows and other country gatherings throughout Cumbria and the Lake District.

This special style is perhaps best described by the "rules".
"The starting backhold position involves the wrestlers standing chest to chest, grasping each other around the body with their chins on their opponent's right shoulder. The right arm of each contestant is positioned above his oponent's left arm. Once the grip is firmly taken, the umpire gives the signal to start the contest by calling "hold". The wrestlers attempt to unbalance their opponent, or make them lose their hold, using any method other than kicking. This is known as a "fall". If any part of a wrestler's body touches the ground aside from his feet, then he loses."

The Grasmere Lift

23

SLATE

Slate is iconic to the Lake District because of its use in so many buildings and stone walls.

We are all aware of slate, which traditionally has been used as one of our main roofing materials. However, in the Lake District, slate is not only found in many of the traditional buildings but it also creates much of the landscape. Technically slate is a type of rock which started life as a shale or mudstone, but which has been metamorphosed (ie transformed by heat and pressure) into the finely cleaved or layered rock we know as slate. Though vast areas of the Lake District are defined as "slate", by no means all of them are of commercial quality. Today, as in the past, slate is quarried, and in some cases mined, at only a few locations.

As well as being used in building, slate is increasingly the chosen natural material for a whole variety of artefacts and things we use about the house, ranging from coffee tables to table mats and house name plaques.

The most spectacular visit to slate workings in the Lake District is located at Honister Slate Mine, at the top of Honister Pass, between Borrowdale and Buttermere Valley. Here you can explore a working slate mine and hear the story of slate.
Telephone: 017687 77230
www.honister-slate-mine.co.uk

Decorative use of slate at Honister Slate Mine

The road to the slate mine

PEOPLE

The people who made their mark on the lake District are highly varied, ranging from the romantic writers and poets of the nineteenth century, to Britain's most famous huntsman and UK's best known writer of walking guides.

Alfred Wainwright

I wandered lonely as a cloud
That floats on high o'er vales and hills
When all at once I saw a crowd,
A host of golden daffodils;
Beside the lake, beneath the trees,
Fluttering and dancing in the breeze.

Continuous as the stars that shine
And twinkle in the Milky Way,
They stretched in never-ending line
Along the margin of the bay;
Ten thousand saw I at a glance,
Tossing their heads in sprightly dance.

The waves beside them danced; but they
Out-did the sparkling waves in glee:
A poet could not but be gay,
In such a jocund company;
I gazed and gazed but little thought
What wealth the show to me had brought:

For oft, when on my couch I lie
In vacant or in pensive mood,
They flash upon that inward eye
Which is the bliss of solitude;
And then my heart with pleasure fills,
And dances with the daffodils.

Glencoyne daffodils today

WORDSWORTH'S DAFFODILS

Wordsworth's poem , "I wandered lonely as a cloud" is possibly the best-known poem in the English language. The first verse, with "a host of golden daffodils……..fluttering and dancing in the breeze" is known by millions of former students.

In April 1802 Wordsworth and his sister Dorothy wandered by Ullswater in the vicinity of Glencoyne, just north of Glenridding, and came across a great swathe of daffodils which almost certainly inspired the iconic poem which was published in 1807 and then in revised version eight years later.

Dorothy kept a journal, and recorded the walk of 15th April 1802 as follows: "I never saw daffodils so beautiful. They grew among the mossy stones, some rested their heads upon these stones as on a pillow for weariness and the rest tossed and reeled and danced and seemed as if they verily laughed with the wind that blew upon them over the lake…"

Wordsworth also wrote three poems about Lakeland's best-known waterfall, Aira Force, which is located just a few kilometres north of Glencoyne on the same side of the lake.

Wordsworth's daffodils today

From the last weeks of March into April each year, the daffodils Dorothy Wordsworth wrote about at Glencoyne bay may still be seen. The flowers are smaller and less spectacular than the massed civic displays we have now become used to in our parks and along our dual carriageways, but they still make a beautiful spectacle against the backdrop of the trees, mosses and the lake.

How to get to the daffodils
Grid reference NY387182
On the lakeside section of the A592 between Glenridding and the junction with the A5091, there is a small patch of gently sloping, open woodland between road and lake, with one parking spot taking about four cars on the lake side. Here you will find Wordsworth's daffodils. See map on page 41.

HOW TO GET THERE
Grid reference NY 342 070
Grasmere is on the A591 road which connects Ambleside with Keswick and the North Lakes. Dove Cottage and the Wordsworth Museum are situated just off the main road at the south end of the village. St Oswald's churchyard is situated in Grasmere village 500 metres northwest of Dove Cottage.

Rydal Mount lies just north of the A591, mid-way between Ambleside and Grasmere. There is limited parking. During the peak season all these locations will be very busy. Early morning or late afternoon may be best. Postcodes: Dove Cottage LA22 9SQ, Rydal Mount LA22 9LU. Map on page 61.

WORDSWORTH'S GRASMERE

Dove Cottage in Grasmere is almost certainly the most famous and most visited house in the Lake District. Wordsworth lived here from 1799 until 1808 and it was here that he wrote much of his poetry.

The house was originally an inn, called the Dove and Olive and was built in the early 1600s. The inn closed in 1793 and it was well after the Wordsworths left that the name Dove Cottage was first applied.

From 1802 onwards, when William married Mary Hutchinson, this was Wordsworth's marital home, and their three eldest children were born here. In 1808 the Wordsworths moved to a larger house, Allan Bank in Grasmere, but stayed there only a few years, losing both their younger children in a place they found cold and damp. They moved to Rydal Mount a few miles towards Ambleside in 1813, where William lived until his death in 1850. Rydal Mount was the biggest and finest house the Wordsworths lived in, and much of it is open to the public today. When he died in 1850 he was regarded as perhaps the world's greatest poet. He was buried in a simple grave in St Oswald's churchyard, Grasmere, marked only by a plain plaque.

Today Dove Cottage is the principal "shrine" to Lakeland's favourite poet. The Wordsworth Trust was founded in 1891, with the objective of securing Dove Cottage for the nation. In 1981 the trust opened a museum which exhibited paintings and manuscripts from a range of the British Romantics, and in 2004 the Jerwood Centre was opened, to provide a facility for conservation, research and a long-term home for trust's outstanding collection.

Opening times
Dove Cottage
9.30 - 17.00 all year. May be closed January for annual maintenance. Charges, with family tickets available. www.wordsworth.org.uk
Rydal Mount
May to Oct: 9.30 - 17.00 daily
Winter: Wed - Sun, 11.00 - 16.00
Charges, with concessions and family tickets.

Rydal Mount

Wordsworth's birth place, Cockermouth

D'ye ken John Peel with his coat so grey,
D'ye ken John Peel at the break of day,
D'ye ken John Peel when he's far (far)
away,
With his hounds and his horn in the
morning.
Chorus
T'was the sound of his horn called me from
my bed
And the cry of his hounds has me oft-times
led,
Peel's "view halloa" would awaken the
dead
Or the fox from his lair in the morning.
D'ye ken that bitch whose tongue was
death?
D'ye ken her sons of peerless faith?
D'ye ken that fox, with his last breath
Curs'd them all as he died in the morning?
Yes I ken John Peel and Ruby too,

Ranter and Royal and Bellman as true,
From the drag to the chase, from the chase
to the view
From a view to the death in the morning.
And I've followed John Peel both often
and far,
O'er the rasper fence and the gate and the
bar,
From low Denton Holme up to Scratch-
more Scar,
Where we view for the brush in the
morning.
Then here's to John Peel with my heart
and soul
Come fill-fill to him another strong bowl,
And we'll follow John Peel through fair
and through foul
While we're waked by his horn in the
morning.

JOHN PEEL

Because of the song *D'ye ken John Peel*, John Peel is probably the Lake District's most famous historical character. Born near the northern Lakeland village of Caldbeck, in approximately 1776, he married one Mary White, whose parents provided a farm for the newly-weds at Ruthwaite, between Ireby and Uldale on the northern edge of today's national park.

Peel was undoubtedly something of a rascal, neglecting his farm, getting seriously into debt and spending much of his time drinking, and, of course, hunting. He has become famous through the song written about his hunting by his friend John Woodcock Graves, who came from Wigton, a few miles further north.

The song
D'ye ken John Peel was originally based on a Scottish dance tune called "Bonnie Annie" and was written in Cumbrian dialect. There have been several versions of the tune, but it is believed that the tune we use today is similar to the original.

John Peel died in a hunting accident in 1854, and his grave in Caldbeck churchyard is possibly one of the most popular tourist sites at the northern end of the national park.

John Peel's grave in Caldbeck

Next to the church in Caldbeck is Priest's Mill, a lovely conversion which houses the Watermill Café, one of Lakeland's best teashops, "The Wool Clip", an outlet for a local co-operative, Neil M Edgar, the Caldbeck jeweller and "Mill Gifts", selling cards and books. There is a wide range of personal artefacts associated with the famous huntsman in Tullie House Museum, next to the castle in Carlisle.
www.tulliehouse.co.uk
01228 618718
CA3 8TP

How to get to Caldbeck
Grid reference NY326 399
From the central Lake District, Caldbeck is most easily reached from the A66 from the junction 5km (3 miles) east of Threlkeld, around the north-eastern edge of National Park.

From the west, approach from Castle Inn at the northern end of Bassenthwaite via Uldale.
The grave has one of the only white headstones in the graveyard, and is situated next to the wall, to the left of the path, close to the church.

Born in 1907, no other modern person is more iconic to the Lake District than Alfred Wainwright. He died in 1991 leaving his remarkable set of hand-written and hand-drawn Pictorial Guides, produced between 1952 and 1966. More than anyone he has inspired a love of walking on the fells, and the word "Wainwright" has become synonymous for routes and walks throughout the Lake District, even more so than the term "Munro" in Scotland. The 214 fells described in his Pictorial Guides are now referred to as "Wainwrights".

He was born in Blackburn and had his first experience of the fells at the age of 23, when he came to Windermere with his cousin. He immediately fell in love with the Lake District. and eleven years later moved to Kendal to work in the Borough Treasurer's office. From 1948 until he retired in 1967 he was Kendal Borough Treasurer.

In November 1952 he started on a meticulously planned journey of writing and drawing. His weekends were spent walking in the fells and every weekday evening he completed one page of his Pictorial Guides. It took 13 years to complete the 7 books, which are still amongst the most respected guides for fell-walkers, even today.

In addition he published other guides on the Pennine Way, the Yorkshire Dales, the Coast to Coast Walk, which he founded, together with other guides with Lakeland. He also published books of drawings and sketches, mainly on the Lake District but also including places well beyond Cumbria.

Wainwright's guides are available in almost every shop which sells books in and around the Lake District.

There is a Wainwright Society, which aims to keep alive the things which Alfred Wainwright promoted through his publications.

www.wainwright.org.uk

The Pictorial Guides
1 The Eastern Fells, completed 1955
2 The Far Eastern Fells, completed 1957
3 The Central Fells, completed 1958
4 The Southern Fells, completed 1960
5 The Northern Fells, completed 1962
6 The North Western Fells, completed 1964
7 The Western Fells, completed 1966

How to get to Hill Top

Grid Ref: SD 370 956

From Ambleside-Coniston road A593, turn off at Clappergates on the B5286 to Hawkshead, where you turn left on the B5285 to the well signed car park at Near Sawrey..

Alternatively, take the car ferry across Windermere, starting just south of Bowness. Once you cross the lake, Near Sawrey is about 2km (1.25 miles) on the B5285. See map on page 75. Hill Top Farm is open to the public and much of the house is as it was left. Telephone: 015394 36 269. Post Code: LA22 0LF

Expect it to be very busy during the high season.

Hill Top, where Beatrix Potter did much of her writing

BEATRIX POTTER

Beatrix Potter was the author of the English-speaking world's most popular series of books for young children, the illustrated stories of characters such as Peter Rabbit, Mrs Tiggy-winkle and Mr Jeremy Fisher. She lived in the Lake District for most of her adult life and when she died owned 4000 acres, mainly in southern Lakeland, and 14 farms, most of which now belong to the National Trust.

Beatrix Potter was born in London in 1866 and developed a love of the countryside from long childhood holidays, first to Perthshire and then to the Lake District. When she was 16 she came with her family to stay at Wray Castle, on the western shore of Windermere, and became friends with the vicar of Wray, Canon H Rawnsley, one of the co-founders of the National Trust, who later became a great source of encouragement in her decision to publish her first book.

Beatrix was an outstanding artist, and during her visits she carefully observed animals and nature, making many sketches, which she later developed into greetings cards and eventually her first book, "The Tale of Peter Rabbit". Although Frederick Warne eventually became her publisher, as with many budding authors, Beatrix' literary efforts initially faced rejection, and she first published "The Tale of Peter Rabbit" privately in 1901 at a cost of £11 for 250 copies.

Her books were an immediate success and in 1905 she was able to use her mounting royalties to buy Hill Top, the farm near Sawrey where she was to do much of her writing. She married the Hawkshead solicitor who acted in her purchases, and bought numerous properties, becoming a conservationist farmer, specialising in the breeding of the Lakeland sheep, the Herdwick.

Near Sawrey

She died in December 1943 as the writer of the world's most famous collection of story books for small children.

They include:
The Tale of Peter Rabbit
The Tale of Squirrel Nutkins
The Tale of Benjamin Bunny
The Tale of Mr Jeremy Fisher
The Story of Miss Moppet
The Tale of Jemima Puddle Duck
The Tale of Johnny Town Mouse...plus many others.

There is also an official Beatrix Potter exhibition, The World of Beatrix Potter at The Old Laundry, Crag Brow, Windermere, LA23 3BX, on the road down to Bowness and the lake.
www.hop-skip.jump.com

BLUEBIRD AND DONALD CAMPBELL

On the morning of 4th January 1967 the usual peace of Coniston on a calm winter morning was shattered by the scream of a jet engine, as Donald Campbell's Bluebird K7 sped across the water at over 300 mph. But this was for the last time; on its second run, Bluebird flipped and cart-wheeled, killing Campbell instantly, and sinking to the bottom of the lake where it stayed until recovery of both boat and body in 2001.

The original Bluebird

Donald Campbell was the son of a famous father, Sir Malcolm Campbell, who, during the 1920s and 1930s, in both cars and boats, held 13 different world speed records. When Malcolm Campbell died, in 1948, Donald, assisted by his father's chief engineer, Leo Villa, took over the mantle, and set about improving both the water and land speed records.

During the 1950s and 60s Campbell increased the water speed record to 202.15 mph on Ullswater in 1955 to over 270mph in Western Australia in 1964. In July 1964 he took the land speed record to over 400mph and became the only man to hold both land and water speed records at the same time.

In December 1966 and January 1967, Coniston provided the location for an attempt to raise the water speed record to over 300mph, and was to result in Donald Campbells's death. The Ruskin Museum in Coniston tells the story and is home to much Bluebird memorabilia. Parts of Bluebird recovered from the lake in 2001 are on display, and shortly, a rebuilt, full-sized working Bluebird will be housed in the museum.
Telephone: 015394 41164

Part of the exhibition at Ruskin Museum

How to get there
The Ruskin Museum is located just off the A593 near the centre of the village of Coniston, which can be accessed either from Ambleside or from the south lakes road, the A590(T).
See map on page 63.

NORTH LAKES

The icons of the North Lakes largely represent the wealth of beautiful and inspirational landscape, many of them featuring in the poetry and writings of the famous nineteenth century romantics and philosophers, such as Wordsworth and Ruskin.

Castlerigg Stone Circle, near Keswick

ASHNESS BRIDGE

Ashness Bridge is among the handful of most-photographed locations in the Lake District. The juxtaposition of an ancient packhorse bridge, the Ashness Beck, a glimpse of Derwentwater, and Skiddaw filling the background, with the whole scene framed by trees gives one of Lakeland's guaranteed photos. What is always described as a "packhorse bridge" is just adequate for a car, and there is parking just beyond.

The view has been photographed a million times, but each photograph is different, depending on the season, the time of day, the weather and where you take the picture from.

Further up the road there is a lovely viewpoint from which you can look on to Derwentwater, Skiddaw and the northern fells. Then continue up the road to one of Lakeland's most accessible and lovely tarns at Watendlath.

Ashness Bridge looking towards Skiddaw

How to get there

Grid reference NY 270196

Start in Keswick at the main car park to the west of the main street. Head for Borrowdale on the B5289. After about 3km (2 miles), take the minor road to the left which goes to Watendlath. Take care as the road is narrow, and may be very busy during the holiday season. You will clearly recognise the bridge only a few hundred metres up the hill. Cross it and park 50 metres on the right. Looking back over the bridge towards Derwentwater and Skiddaw to the north, the view is unmistakeable. See map on page 51.

HOW TO GET THERE
Grid reference NY400 200
The Aira Force National Trust car park (free to members) is located on the A592 on the south-western shores of Ullswater, just east of the junction with the A5091. Both roads allow access from the A66 to the north. Alternatively approach from Ambleside or Windermere over Kirkstone Pass and the A592. In the spring, combine this visit with one to Wordsworth's daffodils, just along the road at Glencoyne bay.

AIRA FORCE

Aira Force is Lakeland's most visited waterfall. Since 1906 it has been owned by the National Trust and the car park on the shores of Ullswater leads to a circular woodland path which takes in Aira Force and High Force, both on the Aira Beck.

Because of its popularity the site can be crowded at weekends at any time of year and especially during holiday periods. Early morning or evening may be best.

Aira Force has been popular for over 200 years and is the subject of three Wordsworth poems.

The falls are about 70 feet high and are located in a beautiful woodland setting, literally created by the Howard family who, in 1780, began landscaping the area with enormous tree plantings, paths and bridges.

In 1846 the Howards planted over 200 specimen conifers, from locations all over the world, with many of the trees planted then becoming the forest giants we see today.

"Simple Map" showing location of Aira Force, Glencoyne Woods, Glenridding and Ullswater Steamers

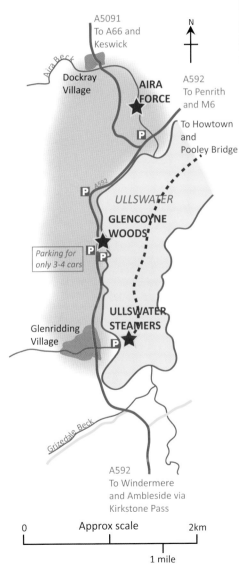

The Somnambulist

"... .how softly then
Doth Aira-force, that torrent hoarse,
Speak from the woody glen!
Fit music for a solemn vale!
And holier seems the ground
To him who catches on the gale
The spirit of a mournful tale,
Embodied in the sound."

Wordsworth 1833

41

How to get there

The Bowder Stone is located just south of Grange village in Borrowdale. Grid Ref NY 254 164.

There is a National Trust car park adjacent to the road, and the stone is a 600 metre, wheelchair-friendly walk.

A wooden stairway allows you to clamber over the rock, though this would not be safe for smaller children.

To find out more

Refer to "The Story of the Bowder Stone" by Alan Smith, published by Rigg Side Publications.

THE BOWDER STONE

The Bowder Stone has been regarded as "something to behold", one of nature's marvels, since tourists began visiting the Lakes and was already famous in the late 1700s.

18 by 8 metres, at an estimated weight of about 1600 or so tonnes, it is one of Britain's biggest free-standing boulders. The stone appears to be delicately balanced, and in immediate danger of falling over. Books and websites perpetuate the myth that it is a glacial erratic, mysteriously brought to Borrowdale from southern Scotland, against the flow of the ice, during the last glaciation. However, more informed geological opinion confirms that the fine grained basalt called andesite, which makes the stone, is of the same origin as the Borrowdale volcanic rocks of Hell's Wall, which tower above to the east. In other words, at some time at the end of the last ice age, about 10,000 years ago, this huge boulder was dislodged from the crag-face by the process of repeated "freeze and thaw" and came tumbling down to the valley below.

The origins of the name are similarly debated. The author favours Diana Whaley's suggestion that it is simply Cumbrian dialect for "boulder". Others associate the name with Balder, son of the Norse God Odin. No doubt debate will continue.

The Bowder Stone and the land around it was one of the first gifts to the National Trust. In 1910 Princess Louise, daughter of Queen Victoria, bought the area of land including the stone as a memorial to the recently-died Edward VII and gave it to the National Trust as one of its first Lake District acquisitions.

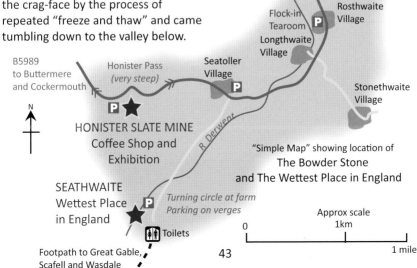

B5989 from Keswick

P 600m walk from car park

★ BOWDER STONE

Rosthwaite Village

Flock-in Tearoom P

Longthwaite Village

B5989 to Buttermere and Cockermouth

Honister Pass *(very steep)*

Seatoller Village P

Stonethwaite Village

N

P ★ HONISTER SLATE MINE Coffee Shop and Exhibition

R. Derwent

"Simple Map" showing location of
The Bowder Stone
and The Wettest Place in England

SEATHWAITE Wettest Place in England

P Turning circle at farm Parking on verges

★

Toilets

Footpath to Great Gable, Scafell and Wasdale

Approx scale 1km

0   1km

1 mile

43

Castlerigg Stone Circle

Castlerigg Stone Circle

Castlerigg Stone Circle was one of the earliest acquisitions of the National Trust and has been amongst Lakeland's most iconic visitor locations since tourists first started their northerly trek to Keswick.

Castlerigg is one of the most complete of the Lake District's 50 or so stone circles, and is visually stunning, set in an amphitheatre of hills and mountains. It has 38 stones, some weighing as much as 16 tonnes, and, at 5,200 years old, is one of the most ancient stone circles in Europe, older than the Great Pyramids of Egypt.

It is also one of the most accessible circles, set on a low plateau just east of Keswick.

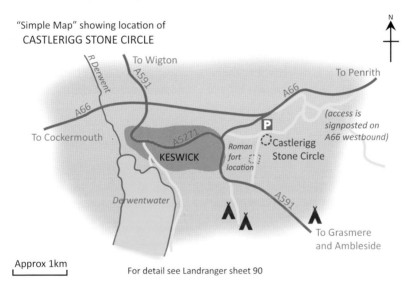

"Simple Map" showing location of
CASTLERIGG STONE CIRCLE

Approx 1km

For detail see Landranger sheet 90

HOW TO GET THERE

From Keswick drive out via the A591, the road to Thirlmere and Ambleside. Turn left on to the road that leads to the A66 for Penrith. Almost immediately, Castlerigg is signposted to the right. The stone circle is about a mile up this road on your right. This is also one of the few circles which is well signposted.

You can also approach from Threlkeld via St John's in the Vale to the east, following the signposts off the A66 from both east and west. The circle is located on a plateau at just over 200 metres, with the Lakeland fells all around. During the holiday season Castlerigg is usually busy. An ice-cream van keeps visitors happy during the "season". Early morning is good, but there are those who park up all night, especially to catch sunset and sunrise.

CUMBERLAND PENCILS

Until the arrival of the anonymous "felt pen", most children in Britain made their initial acquaintance with the Lake District through the picture on a box of coloured pencils, made by the Cumberland Pencil Company of Keswick.

It is believed that graphite, the important constituent in simple "lead" pencils, was discovered at Seathwaite at the head of Borrowdale during the early 1500s, and that shepherds used it to mark their sheep. Britain's first pencil factory was established at Keswick in 1832 and eventually became the Cumberland Pencil Company in 1916, with the launch of the iconic children's range Lakeland in 1930, and the Derwent artists' range starting in 1938. And so began one of the world's most famous ranges of pencils, and the reason for which most adults in UK will know of Keswick.

Production was originally on a site beside the River Greta as you enter Keswick from the west, but has now been transferred to a new factory in Workington. What is left for the visitor, housed in the former factory laboratory, is the Cumberland Pencil Museum, which explains the history of pencil-making and how pencils are made. Sketchers Coffee Shop gives you time to re-fuel, while the kids are enjoying the Drawing Zone.

A colourful array of pencils

How to get there
Grid reference NY263 237
Arrive from the A66 junction which has a roundabout with the A591. Head towards Keswick, about 800 metres (0.5 mile). At a T-junction turn left, cross the river and immediately turn left into the former pencil factory site. The museum is clearly sign-posted. The main town centre in Keswick, plus the main parking, Lake Derwent Water etc are only another 100 metres or so into the town.

THE BISHOP

In 1783 the newly appointed Bishop of Londonderry was travelling from Keswick to Whitehaven, when he stopped for the night in the Swan Inn at Thornthwaite on the shores of Bassenthwaite. After a session of heavy drinking the bishop wagered (possibly with his clerk)) that he could ride his pony to the summit of the nearby fell, called The Barf. A few hundred feet up, he and his pony both fell to their deaths. Since then, the rock at which they fell has been called "The Bishop" and has been whitewashed annually by the staff of the Swan Inn. Sadly, the Swan Inn has now closed and has been converted into flats. Hopefully the new flat-owners will keep up the tradition.

HOW TO FIND IT

Grid reference NY 217 265

You will see the Bishop most easily travelling on the A66 northwards along the western side of Bassenthwaite. Although the Swan Inn is now closed, there is parking from which you can view the Bishop.

It is possible to reach the rock, although it involves a stiff climb, much of it on loose scree, and the "white-washers" have done so annually. But remember, if the story is correct, both bishop and pony fell to their deaths there!

The Bishop, on the western shores of Bassenthwaite

HOW TO GET THERE
Grid reference NY263 222
In Keswick, park in the large car park next to the theatre. This is accessed from the main town, following signs for the lake. Head for the lake, which is beyond the theatre. It is possible to walk along the shore, past the rowing boats and launches, but best follow the marked path for about 500 metres. Take photographs either from the crag itself or to get the iconic shot which includes the crag and the lake, retrace your steps and branch off the path to the little bay below the crag.

See map on page 51.

Friar's Crag

Along with Ashness Bridge, not far away, Friar's Crag must be one of the most photographed locations in the Lake District. The poet John Ruskin thought it one of the most beautiful places on earth.

The crag is a low, rocky peninsula 500 metres south of the Keswick jetties on Derwent Water, giving fine views of the lake, its islands and the fells beyond. Inevitably its name is the stuff of legend, and is most certainly ancient. The most southerly island in Derwent Water is named St Herbert's Island, reputedly after the hermit monk, Herbert, who lived there in the 7th century. He was a disciple of St Cuthbert, bishop of Lindisfarne on Holy Island, off the Northumberland coast. The legend suggests that fellow monks would signal from the crag of their intent to bring supplies, and so the name began. After Herbert's death, the island became a place of pilgrimage, and the journey across would start at Friar's Crag.

The poet Ruskin came here in 1824 as a boy of five. He was so impressed that he later wrote of his visit as "the creation of the world for me".

Friar's Crag was bought by the National Trust in 1901, as a result of the Trust's first-ever large appeal.

Friar's Crag is almost always busy. To try and ensure a quieter time, go early in the morning or in the evening.

As with nearby Ashness Bridge your photo will be one of millions, but depending on weather, season and time of day, it will be unique.

View from Friar's Crag

How to get there
Grid reference NY 264 228
The Keswick jetty is easy to find,
situated only a few hundred metres
from the town centre, off the B5289
Borrowdale road. Park in the large car
park next to the theatre.
For other jetties, see map.

Derwent Island and Catbells

KESWICK LAUNCHES

Derwentwater is the shallowest of the lakes, and retains the traditional lakes launches, allowing visitors a taste of how it has been for many decades. The launches carry about 25 passengers and run every half hour around the lake, starting from Keswick pier, with clockwise cruises on the hour, and anti-clockwise cruises on the half hour. The round trip takes 50 minutes, but it is possible to disembark at 7 different landing stages around the lake. Derwentwater is beautifully situated, with the rugged fells of the Borrowdale volcanic rocks all around to the south, east and west, with the majestic outline of Skiddaw filling the northern horizon.

The Keswick Launch Company was founded in 1935 by Victor Hodgson, Walter Walker and two brothers, Allan and Herbert Birkett. They started with the May Queen, an electric-powered boat, built in 1902, which they bought from the England family at Lodore Hotel. Uniquely, its batteries were charged by a private hydro-electric scheme at the Lodore Falls.

Before the Keswick Launch Company, visitors could be taken around the Derwentwater islands in 16 seater rowing boats.

Borrowdale is full of interest, and although many visitors enjoy the round trip, a good many will take the launch to or from the start or finish of their walk. Ashness jetty gives access to Ashness Bridge and Watendlath Tarn; Lodore to the famous falls; Hawes End

is at the bottom of the famous Catbells. Contacts:
Telephone: 017687 72263
info@keswick-launch.co.uk
www.keswick-launch.co.uk

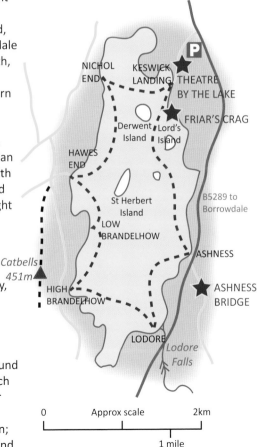

"Simple Map" showing location of Derwentwater Launch Route, Ashness Bridge and Friar's Crag

How to get there
Grid reference of summit NY 260 291
The easiest route for an ascent of
Skiddaw is from the car park north of
Latrigg (Grid reference NY282 254).
Leave the A66 at the roundabout north
of Keswick on to the A591.

Almost immediately, turn right for
Ormathwaite. After about 1 km (just
over ½ mile) turn righ t on to the minor
road just beyond Underscar Hotel. A
further kilometre leads to the car park
which marks the start of the ascent of
Skiddaw.

Skiddaw in springtime

SKIDDAW

We have chosen Skiddaw as the iconic mountain in the northern Lakes not because the author looked out on it every clear day for his first 18 years, but because it is both the most visible and the most accessible of the four tops above 3000 feet.

Skiddaw dominates the northern fells and occupies most of the view as you look out from the Lake District from Keswick. It is very different from the volcanic central fells. Its steep, regular smooth slopes reflect the homogeneous underlying geology of the Skiddaw Slates, a collection of silts, mudstones and sandstones, all in excess of 400 million years. Some of them have been metamorphosed (changed by later heat and pressure) into the slates which characterise the buildings of the area. Wainwright was much impressed by Skiddaw's "massive strength and such beauty of outline."

Standing out from the massif of the central fells, Skiddaw gives an unsurpassed selection of views for those who make the relatively easy ascent. As well as most of the Lake District and the high tops of the Dales, the Isle of Man is clearly visible, as are the Mountains of Mourne in Northern Ireland. You can see Snowdonia, and also into Scotland as far as Goat Fell on the island of Arran, just west of Glasgow.

For a collection of possible ascents, refer to Wainwright,'s "Pictorial Guide to the Lake land Fells", Book 5, The Northern Fells.
Grid reference: NY 260 290 (Landranger 89 & 90)
Altitude: 931 m (3054 ft)
Geology: Skiddaw Slate
Access: Easiest path is from the car park north of Latrigg at NY 282 254.

Skiddaw from Ashness Bridge in November

HOW TO GET THERE
Glenridding is situated at the southwest end of Ullswater on the A592, which is accessible from Penrith off the A66, one mile west of Junction 40 on the M6. From Ambleside and Windermere Ullswater is accessed over Kirkstone Pass on the A592 road, and from Keswick, first on the A66 towards Penrith, then after about 12km (7.5 miles) turn left on to the A5091.
See map on page 41.

ULLSWATER STEAMERS

Ullswater Steamers began in 1859, when the Ullswater Navigation Company began its steamer services, carrying passengers, goods and mail to various locations around the lake. Today four boats still operate, though all are now converted to diesel engines rather than the original steam. Two are well over 100 years old, the Lady of the Lake, launched in 1877 and the Raven, built in 1889.

The main base is Glenridding pier, at the southern end of the lake, and boats ply the lake all year, except for Christmas Eve and Christmas Day. There are stops at Pooley Bridge at the north end of the lake, and at Howtown on the eastern shore. During the summer season there are sailings roughly every 45 minutes.

Ullswater is often described as England's most beautiful lake, and the steamers allow visitors a variety of ways of enjoying the landscape. Some opt for the 2 hour trip around the lake, taking in the full majesty of Ullswater. Others take a short hop from Glenridding to Howtown, on the eastern shore of the lake, and then walk the 7 miles back to Glenridding, or perhaps on to Pooley Bridge.

Check out summer evening buffet cruises or commentary cruises which explore the range of natural and cultural history offered by the lake. And another idea. Looking for a wedding venue? Why not weave a little history into your life and get married on one of these historic boats?

How to find out more
See www.ullswater-steamers.co.uk
E-mail: hello@ullswater-steamers.co.uk
Telephone: 017684 82229

55

HOW TO GET THERE

Grid reference NY 235 122

Seathwaite is at the southern end of Borrowdale, which is accessed either from Keswick or over Honister pass from Buttermere valley, both on the B5289. Head south to Seathwaite just east of the village of Seatoller for about 2km (just over 1 mile) Park alongside the road, making sure not to block the turning space next to the farm. There is a tea-shop, a small trout fishery and there are also some nice waterfalls close by. Taylorgill Force, one of the most spectacular falls in Lakeland, is only a mile up the valley. See map on page 43.

The road to Seathwaite on a May Bank Holiday

WETTEST PLACE IN ENGLAND

There may be wetter, uninhabited places in England, but the wettest place where someone actually lives is Seathwaite at the head of Borrowdale, with an official annual rainfall average of 3552 mm (140 inches).

As every school pupil probably knows, England gets most of its rain from the west, with relatively warm, moisture-laden air from the Atlantic being forced to rise over the Lakeland fells. As it does so it is cooled, reducing the air's capacity to hold water vapour. The result is rain, lots of it, at all seasons. The Lake District is wonderfully beautiful, but it is also incredibly well-watered. Each year usually has about 200 wet days and about 145 dry days. In 1966 one infamous rainstorm produced a record-breaking 5 inches of rain in 5 hours.

The most recent deluge occurred in October 2008 during the Mountain Marathon, when the road to Seathwaite became a river, several feet deep.

Keswick's annual rainfall averages 1470 mm (58 inches). Elsewhere rainfall generally increases with altitude and westerliness.

Seathwaite is a collection of farm buildings, a few cottages and verge-side car park 400 metres long. In the summer it has a tea shop, and there are public toilets and a public telephone.

This is the start of many well-known walks and climbs, and may be on your chosen route to Scafell, Great Gable, or into another valley such as Langdale or Wasdale. Wainwright referred to it as "a pedestrian metropolis". It can be very busy, with parking at a premium during the holiday season, usually extending alongside the road to the hump-backed bridge across the embryonic River Derwent, as shown on the opposite page.

Sour Milk Ghyll, Seathwaite Valley

Seathwaite Farm

THEATRE BY THE LAKE

If you are new to Keswick you will be surprised to find a fine, modern theatre, located on your walk to Friar's Crag or to the Keswick launch pier. Equally, many regular visitors to Keswick will have enjoyed the summer season of a first-class theatre here for almost 50 years.

The Theatre by the Lake

It all started in 1961 with what was affectionately called the "Blue Box Theatre", a sort of travelling theatre "prefab", which housed the Century Theatre Company. Originally the site was where the main high street car park is now located, and from 1976 the "Blue Box" was moved to the present site, just off the road to the lake. In August 1999 the new 400 seat permanent theatre was completed, partly financed by the National Lottery,

and it was opened in December of that year by the theatre's president, Dame Judi Dench.

The theatre runs a summer season of six plays, giving the opportunity for the northern lakes visitors to enjoy a selection of live drama during their holiday. At Christmas there is always a special seasonal production, and there is also something for a spring season. The original pre-fabricated theatre, the "Blue Box", is now in Leicester, still going strong.

How to book
The easiest way to book is online.
www.theatrebythelake.co.uk
Telephone: 017687 74411
By post: Theatre by the Lake, Keswick, CA12 5DJ . Map on page 51

Performers at the theatre

HOW TO GET THERE
Grid reference NY266 228
From central Keswick take the B5289 road for The Lake and Borrowdale. The road to the lake is off to the right after only a few hundred metres. The theatre is located just beyond the large car park, a hundred metres before Derwentwater.

SOUTH LAKES

Many of the South Lakes Icons date from the arrival of the railways in the mid-19th century. This more than anything made steamboats, idyllic landscapes and Lakeland villages all available to the masses for the first time.

Gondola, Coniston Water

How to get there
Grid reference SD 313 959
Located on a minor road on the eastern shore of Coniston Water, accessible either from the Ambleside to Coniston road, B5285 or from the south from the A5092.

Alternatively, during the summer, the perfect way to arrive is via the Victorian steamboat, Gondola, from Coniston pier across the lake.

See map on page 63.

BRANTWOOD

Brantwood is the former home of the Victorian thinker, writer and artist, John Ruskin. Ruskin died in 1900, and its is said that he was responsible, more than any other writer, in shaping the tastes and values of Victorian England. However, it is his home, Brantwood, on the eastern shores of Coniston Water, that we list as a Lake District icon. Brantwood is one of the most splendid visitable houses in Lakeland and few would doubt its claims to be the most beautifully situated house in Cumbria. One can make the visit in a unique way by catching the splendidly appointed National Trust steam yacht Gondola, built in 1859, from the pier at Coniston and arriving in style across the lake.

Ruskin was one of those Victorians who was into everything, art, architecture, criticism and writing, social values and philosophy, and his house and its present use reflects this. Brantwood is full of Ruskin art, furniture and memorabilia. It is used for special events, activities and exhibitions. There are also gardens set in Brantwood's 250 acres estate. "Jumping Jenny" is Brantwood's coffee shop-restaurant.

Contacts
www.brantwood.org.uk
e-mail: enquiries@brantwood.org.uk
Telephone: 015394 41396

Brantwood has gardens full of rhododendrons and azaleas

How to get there

Grid Reference SD 309970
Head to the village of Coniston on the A593, either from Ambleside, or from the South Lakes road A 590(T). On the south side of village is the road to the lake, where there is parking and café and the pier from which Gondola departs.
Telephone: 015394 41288
email: gondola@nationaltrust.org.uk
www.nationaltrust.org/gondola

GONDOLA STEAMBOAT

Since the coming of the railways to Lakeland, in about 1860, steamboats on the lakes have been part of the tradition. On most of the lakes, steam power has given way to diesel engines, but on Coniston, the recently restored steam yacht Gondola still takes tourists around the lake.

Gondola was built in 1859 for the Furness Railway Company to provide an attraction for the tourists which the train brought to Coniston. The boat plied the lake for 77 years, until she was retired in 1936. However, in the 1970s the steamboat was restored and relaunched, to carry visitors around the lake, starting at Coniston pier. The trip proceeds anti-clockwise around the lake, stopping at Brantwood, the former home of Victorian artist and philosopher John Ruskin. From the opulence of the craft, clearly in the 1860s this was a very classy way to travel, and would have been aimed at the very wealthy of the day.

"Simple Map" showing location of the Gondola Pier and Brantwood

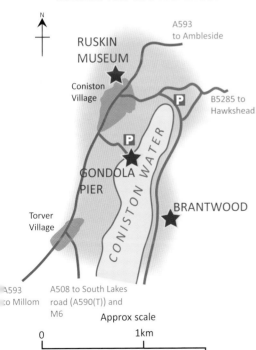

The decorative prow of Gondola

GRASMERE SPORTS

Grasmere Sports day is held on the last Sunday in August. Originally held on the first Tuesday in September, it has taken place in its present form since 1852 and has its origins long in the past.

Today about 10,000 visitors will gather to experience a range of traditional and modern sporting contests and to have a great day out. Traditional events will include Cumberland and Westmorland style wrestling, fell racing (more properly called "guide races"), hound trails, together with more usual athletic events. One of the modern innovations has been the replacement of traditional cycling events with mountain biking.

In addition, expect to find everything associated with the "carnival", including marching bands, dog shows, bouncy castles, bird of prey displays and all manner of stalls selling food and crafts.

Grasmere Sports are very ancient, probably originating in farmers' gatherings or gala days, long before the idea of the modern holiday. The Sports Day is one of the prime venues for Lakeland sporting activities such as Cumberland and Westmorland wrestling, one of the oldest sporting traditions in Europe. (See page 23) Another tradition is the Guides Race, a lung-bursting ascent and seemingly suicidal descent of nearby Butter Crag. The first guides race was held in 1869 and records show the winner as a Mr G Birkett.

The Sports provide a glorious, colourful spectacle, shoe-horned into the only decent piece of flat land in the valley.

Contacts
www.grasmeresportsandshow.co.uk

Gruelling race at Grasmere Sports

Youthful determination

How to get there
Grid reference NY 340 076
Postal Code LA23 9SL
Grasmere is located just off the main
A591 road which runs from Kendal and Windermere through to Keswick.
See map on page 65.

LION AND THE LAMB
or The Old Lady at the Piano?

The Lion and the Lamb is the name traditionally given to the appearance of the rocks at the summit of Helm Crag just north of Grasmere, when viewed from the A591 as you descend Dunmail Raise. However, depending on where you look from, the same rock formation is also referred to as "The Old Lady at the Piano". What do *you* think?

How to get there

Helm Crag Grid reference NY 325 094
View of Lion and the Lamb NY 354 100.
Grasmere village NY 336 075

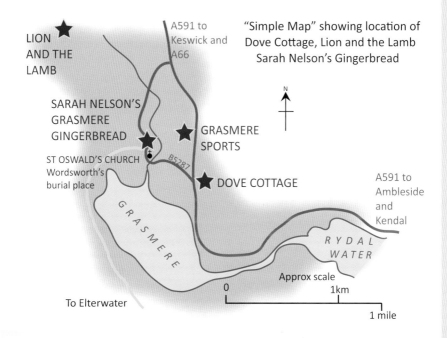

"Simple Map" showing location of Dove Cottage, Lion and the Lamb Sarah Nelson's Gingerbread

LION AND THE LAMB

A591 to Keswick and A66

SARAH NELSON'S GRASMERE GINGERBREAD

GRASMERE SPORTS

ST OSWALD'S CHURCH
Wordsworth's burial place

DOVE COTTAGE

A591 to Ambleside and Kendal

BS287

N

GRASMERE

RYDAL WATER

Approx scale

0   1km

1 mile

To Elterwater

LAKELAND

Mention "Lakeland" and half the population will think of lakes and mountains; the other half, probably mainly ladies, will think of something entirely different, the Lake District's most successful retail company, originating in Windermere and now found at 40 locations throughout the UK.

"Lakeland" was founded in Windermere as Lakeland Plastics during the 1960s by Alan Rayner, then working in animal feedstuffs. Producers of poultry needed a supplier of freezer bags and Alan was the one to supply them. During the 1970s and 80s a company developed which encompassed home freezing and "everything for home cooking". Sons Sam, Martin and Julian took over from their father, and Michelle Kershaw joined the company.

By the 1990s Lakeland Plastics, soon to become Lakeland Ltd, had embraced the internet revolution, with on-line shopping and was becoming a household name throughout the UK..

Today Lakeland has its distribution centre in Kendal. Windermere is the home of its flagship store and restaurant, and the mecca for all those visitors who come to the Lake District not for the lakes but for "Lakeland", and the sort of alternative therapy which is totally beyond the understanding of the author. As inferred earlier, perhaps it's a gender thing.

Lakeland now encompasses an enormous range of products, though the core is still firmly centred on things for the kitchen. A recent innovation is a Lakeland Garden catalogue.

HOW TO GET THERE

Lakeland Ltd is located at the northern end of Windermere town, right next to the railway station, just off the A591 Kendal to Ambleside road. As with all popular locations, it is very busy during the main holiday season, especially at weekends.

SWALLOWS AND AMAZONS

This title will mean nothing to many readers, but will conjure up a world of excitement and childhood adventure for the rest. "Swallows and Amazons" is the first title in a series of children's stories written by Arthur Ransome in 1930. Between then and 1947 he went on to write the Swallows and Amazons series.

The books are set in the Lake District, approximately in the Windermere-Coniston area, although he is never totally specific about locations. Ransome spent his schooldays at Windermere and in his childhood summers enjoyed family holidays at Nibthwaite, south of Coniston. At various times he worked for the Manchester Guardian as a foreign correspondent in St Petersburg, reputedly as a spy, then as a full-time writer, living in the Lake District. Swallows and Amazons was supposedly inspired by a summer which Ransome spent at Lake Coniston, teaching the children of his family friends, the Altounyans, to sail. They had two small dinghies, the Swallow and the Mavis (which became the Amazon in the books), and the Altounyan children became the Walkers: John, Susan, Titty and Roger.

The Swallows and Amazons story takes place on and around a lake which is described as "the great lake in the north". The Walker children meet with another family, the Blacketts, on Wild Cat Island, and undergo a Tom Sawyer-type range of adventures, involving boats, pirates and exploring.

Although it is difficult to identify any particular places in the books, Arthur Ransome insisted that all the locations were actually real, but not necessarily accurate in relation to each other. For many young readers in the 1930s and 40s and later, the stories provided a vision of the Lake District and an inspiration to come and visit, just as powerful in its way as the Romantic poets 100 years previously.

Copy of the "Swallows and Amazons" original cover

SMALLEST HOUSE IN ENGLAND

The Bridge House at Ambleside is almost certainly the most photographed house in the Lake District, and claims to be the smallest house in England. Apart from its size, it is also unusual in being built on top of a bridge, across the Stock beck.

The house was built in the 16th century, initially as an apple store for Ambleside Hall, now demolished. The location on the bridge is said to have been a device for evading land tax. At one time the house is said to have been home for a family of eight.

Apart from its small size and peculiar location, the Bridge House is also famous as having been a subject for the great water-colourist Turner. In 1926 the house was bought by a group of local enthusiasts and donated to the National Trust for its safe keeping. It then became the National Trust's first ever information centre,and is still used by the Trust today.

The house continues to be a much-photographed curio between the car park and the centre of Ambleside.

Bridge House, Ambleside, perched over Stock Beck

How to get there
Grid reference SD375 945
Located on the A591 main road as it leaves Ambleside towards Grasmere. If you park in the main Ambleside car park, you will pass the Bridge House on your way into the centre of town.

HAYES OF AMBLESIDE

At almost any time of year, a large proportion of visitors to the Lake District, especially those who come just for the day, head not for the hills or the lakes but to Hayes Garden World of Ambleside, one of Britain's best-known nurseries.

In these days when garden centres have popped up on the fringes of every town and village in the land, it is interesting to find a garden business which has been literally rooted in southern Lakeland for over 200 years. Just as almost all of the apparently wild rural landscape is actually man-made, so many of the gardens of the southern Lake District owe much to generations of the Hayes family.

The first Hayes gardening brothers began in the early 1800s, encouraged especially by the plethora of large houses which began to sprout in southern Lakeland at this time, increasing with the arrival of the railways in the middle of the century.

Hayes established the Lake District Nurseries on their present site in 1921, on the southern outskirts of Ambleside. In 1987 the present modern expansion began, with the creation of their "Crystal Palace" structure. Today Hayes Garden World is one of the prime visitor destinations in the southern lakes, and together with the outlet in Leeds attracts over 1 million visitors a year.

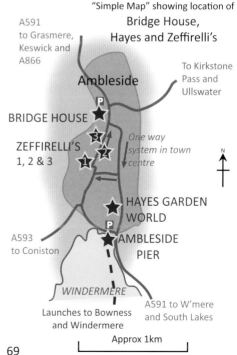

"Simple Map" showing location of **Bridge House, Hayes and Zeffirelli's**

A591 to Grasmere, Keswick and A866

Ambleside

To Kirkstone Pass and Ullswater

BRIDGE HOUSE ★

ZEFFIRELLI'S 1, 2 & 3

One way system in town centre

N

HAYES GARDEN WORLD

A593 to Coniston

AMBLESIDE PIER

WINDERMERE

A591 to W'mere and South Lakes

Launches to Bowness and Windermere

Approx 1km

How to get there
Grid reference NY 377 035
On A591, south side of Ambleside.
www.hayesgardenworld.co.uk
Telephone: 015394 33434

How to get to there
The usual access is from the A593, Ambleside to Coniston road, leaving for Great Langdale and Elterwater at Skelwith Bridge, only 2 km (3 miles) west of Ambleside.
Or alternatively, visitors from west Cumbria can approach via the dramatic Hardknott and Wrynose passes from Eskdale.

LANGDALE PIKES

Visible from numerous locations, including the popular Tarn Hows, the view of the rugged Langdale Pikes is probably the best loved mountain scene of the southern lakes. We include the Langdales because they are stunning and unmistakable. Wainwright was especially enthusiastic, mainly because of the dramatic and rapid rocky rise in altitude from Great Langdale to the summits over a very short distance.

There are three summits in the Langdale Pikes, Harrison Stickle, Pike of Stickle and Loft Crag. These fells feature in some of the earliest evidence we have of man's life in the Lake District.

Axes formed from the rocks on the scree below Pike of Stickle have been found all over Britain, and were possibly traded at Lakeland's number one stone circle, Castlerigg, about 5000 years ago.

The Pikes owe their iconic status to being highly visible, not only from Ambleside and Windermere, but from all approaches to the southern Lake District. They are relatively easy to climb, usually from Great Langdale or from further away locations such as Grasmere or even Stonethwaite at the southern end of Borrowdale. Guidebooks and web pages offer a host of different routes.

Langdale Pikes from Great Langdale

Opposite page - Langdale Pikes from Tarn Hows in winter

Wheelchair-friendly path round Tarn Hows

TARN HOWS

The spectacularly beautiful Tarn Hows is one of the most popular visitor locations in the entire Lake District, so try and go during the low season, (autumn is lovely) or if you must be there in the high season, try early morning or in the evening.

Tarn Hows, far from typical of Lake District scenery, is largely man-made, and is mainly surrounded by non-native conifers. However, the intricate shape of several tarns now made into one,

the constantly varying hues of the trees, and the backdrop of Lakeland fells combine to make a lovely cameo, especially in autumn.

The tarn and the surrounding area is in the care of the National Trust and was originally owned by Beatrix Potter, the iconic children's story writer (see page 34-35).

There are some lovely walks, including a 2km (1.5 mile) wheelchair-friendly circular walk around the tarn.

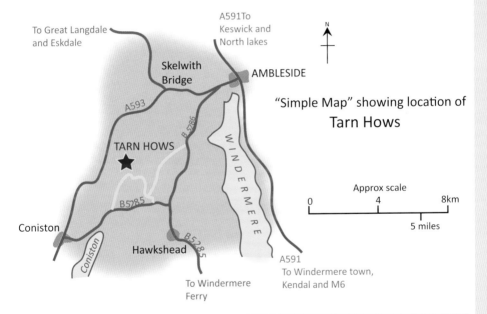

"Simple Map" showing location of **Tarn Hows**

How to get there
Grid reference SD330999.
A detailed route description will be confusing, as it is accessed along a myriad of country lanes. Tarn Hows is located in the triangle formed by Ambleside, Hawkshead and Coniston.

Head along the A593, between Coniston and Ambleside, from either direction, and look out for the signposts to "Tarn Hows".
It may be very busy, with city drivers struggling with very narrow country roads.

How to get there

Bowness Pier: Post Code LA23 3HQ
Grid reference: SD 401 968
Ambleside Pier: Post Code LA22 0EY
Grid reference: SD 376 031
Lakeside Pier: Post Code LA12 8AS
Grid reference: SD 378 874

Bowness is reached via the A591 (Junction 36 on the M6). Lakeside is reached via the A590, signposted at Newby Bridge, also from Jct 36 on M6.
Contact Information:
Telephone: 015394 43057
www.windermere-lakecruises.co.uk

WINDERMERE LAKE CRUISES

If you have only done one thing in the Lake District, apart from walking and climbing, it is most likely to have been a cruise on Windermere, reportedly the most popular single visitor attraction. There are three main starting points for a cruise. Bowness is in the centre of the lake, on the east bank; Ambleside is at the north end, and Lakeside is in the south-west corner. Around the lake there are other stopping off points such as Wray Castle. In addition there is a vehicle ferry from just south of Bowness across the lake. One attractive possibility, for a whole day out, is to "Park and Sail", leaving your car at Lakeside for the whole day for only a few pounds.

There is a wide variety of vessels, ranging from MV Teal and MV Swan, each taking over 500 passengers, to the small, traditional, wooden lake launches which only take about 25 people. Depending on where you are staying, there are all sorts of options.

* Cruise down to Bowness from Ambleside and enjoy a day's shopping

* Combine a lake cruise with a trip on the Lakeside-Haverthwaite steam railway.

* Stop off at Wray Castle for a walk in Lakeland's biggest forest at Grisedale.

* Or organise a special trip for business, dinner afloat, or even to get married! Check out the website.

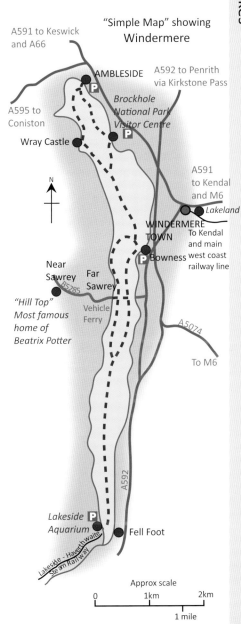

"Simple Map" showing Windermere

A591 to Keswick and A66

AMBLESIDE
A592 to Penrith via Kirkstone Pass

Brockhole National Park Visitor Centre

A595 to Coniston

Wray Castle

A591 to Kendal and M6

Lakeland

WINDERMERE TOWN
To Kendal and main west coast railway line

Bowness

Near Sawrey
B5285
Far Sawrey

"Hill Top"
Most famous home of Beatrix Potter

Vehicle Ferry

A5074

To M6

A592

Lakeside Aquarium

Fell Foot

Lakeside - Haverthwaite Steam Railway

Approx scale

0   1km   2km

1 mile

75

ZEFFIRELLIS

During the 1960s, along with the railways, most small towns in England lost their local cinema. So it was throughout Cumbria, except in Ambleside, where cinema not only continued but has thrived.

Derek Hook took over the Ambleside Cinema in 1982, called it Zeffirellis after the famous Italian film-director and over the years, with the rest of the Hook family, has transformed it into a four-screen cinema, a Friday/Saturday evening Jazz Bar, and a restaurant and café. Big city culture in small-town Ambleside.

The original site in Compston Road, has two screens, both with Dolby surround sound systems and induction loops, and screen 1 with new, state of the art digital projection. Screens 3 and 4 are at Zeffs in the Park, off the same road, just 100 metres away, both with Dolby sound, and screen 3 with brand-new digital projection. Together, Zeffirellis four screens cater for the widest range of cinema, from the latest movies to Arthouse, foreign language and special interest films.

Zeffirellis also offers the famous "Movie Deal", combining a two-course dinner with a reserved cinema seat, all for an inclusive price. Food is simple, Mediterranean, vegetarian and not without a hint of flair. During the day Zeffirellis Café is open for coffee and lunch.

Zeffirellis' Jazz Bar completes the treat, offering a range of artists usually only found in venues such as Ronnie Scott's in London. Many events are free and can be enjoyed with a meal and a drink, making for a fantastic evening out.

All in all Zeffirellis is an unexpected splash of art and culture, thriving in the southern Lake District. On your holiday enjoy the beauty of Lakeland during the day, and something entirely different in the evenings.

Contacts
Bookings: 015394 33845
E-mails: enquiries@zeffirellis.com
www.zeffirellis.com

How to get there
Venues are on Compston Road and Lake Road. See map on page 69. The main Ambleside car park is off the road out to Grasmere and Keswick. Postal code: LA22 9AD Screens 1 and 2, and LA22 9DJ Screens 3 and 4.

KENDAL MINT CAKE

Along with Cumberland Sausages, Kendal Mint Cake is the iconic food item of the Lake District, and because of its history, has almost magical energy-giving connotations.

For those who are uninitiated, Kendal Mint Cake is a mint-flavoured sugar confectionery, sold in a bar. According to Romneys, its present manufacturers, it has "a subtle but stimulating flavour, cool in summer, fiery in winter, and has a unique blend of textures, smooth and hard, but always creamy when sucked". The product is said to have originated in Kendal in a recipe developed by accident by a local confectioner, a Mr Wiper during the 1860s. Kendal Mint Cake first came to fame when it was supplied to Shackleton's 1914-1917 Transarctic Expedition.

Most importantly Kendal Mint Cake was also supplied to the British Everest Expedition which became the first to climb Mt Everest in May 1953. Sir Edmund Hillary and Sherpa Tensing ate Kendal Mint Cake on the summit of Everest and Tensing also left mint cake at the top of the mountain as an offering. And, as they say, the rest is history.

The company was run by Harry Wiper until 1987, when it was bought by George Romney Ltd, who today still maintain the traditional recipe and methods of manufacture.

Visitors can buy Kendal Mint Cake everywhere in the Lake District and at confectioners throughout UK.

sales@kendal.mintcake.co.uk

SARAH NELSON'S GRASMERE GINGERBREAD

Sarah Kemp was born in Windermere in 1815. She married Wilfred Nelson, a farm labourer in 1844, supplementing the meagre family income by baking for Lady Farquhar in Grasmere. About 1850 the former school building then known as Gates Cottage became available for rent, and the house became the base for Sarah Nelson to bake gingerbread and cakes for the ever-growing number of tourists flocking to the Lake District. Sarah's gingerbread became renowned and her recipe was kept a closely guarded secret. When Sarah died, aged 88, in 1904, the recipe was passed to her great niece, who sold it to Daisy Hotson. Daisy later went into business with Jack and Mary Wilson, and the business has remained with the Wilson family ever since.

The famous gingerbread is sold in the same tiny shop, next to the church, and nowhere else.

Open: Mon- Sat: 9.00 - 5.30
              Sundays: 12.30 - 5.30
Make a day of it, and visit Wordsworth's Dove Cottage and Rydal Mount on the same trip.
Contacts: 015394 35428
www.grasmeregingerbread.co.uk

How to get there
Grid reference NY 336 075
Post Code LA22 9SW. Map on Page 65. Sarah Nelson's is located in the centre of Grasmere village, next to St Oswald's church, where William Wordsworth is buried. The village is just off the A591, 5km (3 miles) north of Ambleside.

The "serving girls" at Sarah Nelson's Gingerbread shop

WEST LAKES

The West is generally more remote, has fewer visitors and we have chosen only two icons. Wastwater is wild and awe-inspiring, and the Ravenglass-Eskdale railway is one of Britain's favourite miniature lines.

"River Irt" at Dalegarth Terminus

HOW TO GET THERE

Grid reference SD 085 965
The Ravenglass and Eskdale Railway terminus and museum are situated just off the main west coast road, A595 (T) roughly midway between Whitehaven and Millom. For most, the A595 will provide the easiest access. You can also approach Eskdale via the spectacular Hardnott and Wrynose Passes, the eastern end of the route starting from the A593 near Ambleside, just east of Skelwith Bridge. It is also possible to arrive at Ravenglass by mainline train.

RAVENGLASS AND ESKDALE RAILWAY

The Ravenglass and Eskdale Railway affectionately known as "L'arle Ratty", opened in May 1875 to carry iron ore from near Boot in Eskdale to Ravenglass on the coast. At 3 feet, the track gauge was wider than the 15 inch gauge today. The railway then underwent an eventful ninety or so years, including bankruptcy and the collapse of several businesses, until in 1960 it began to take on its present form as one of the Lake District's most loved tourist attractions.

The railway line begins its journey next to the sea at Ravenglass, the only spot where the Lake District National Park reaches the coast. From there it heads along Miterdale, the valley of the River Mite, hugging the northern edge of Muncaster Fell towards Irton. From there the line follows the northern side of Eskdale as far as Dalegarth station, just short of the village of Boot, a total of 13 km (about 7 miles).

Apart from the spectacular scenery of one of the more remote parts of the National Park, the train journey gives you the possibility of the thrill of riding behind a real steam engine. There are currently four steam engines operating, including River Irt, (built 1894) the oldest 15 inch gauge steam engine in the world still in operation, and Northern Rock (built 1976), one of the world's most powerful 15 inch gauge locomotives. Other, currently non-operational, locomotives can be viewed in the museum.

Some trains will be hauled by diesel engines, so if steam is important to you, check before you go.

Contacts
www.ravenglass-railway.co.uk
steam@ravenglass-railway.co.uk
01229 717171

"Simple Map" showing location of Ravenglass to Eskdale Railway

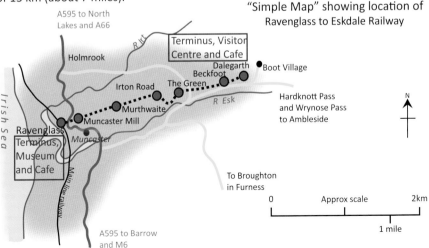

How to get there
Grid ref: NX 183 076 (Wasdale Head Campsite)
Post Code: CA20 1EX (Campsite)
Usual access point from the north is via Gosforth on the A595(T) main west coast route. From Gosforth take the road (unclassified) to Nether Wasdale and the south-western end of the lake. The road continues to Wasdale Head, a mile beyond the head of the lake.
From the south, turn off the A595(T) at Holmrook and head for Santon.

WASTWATER
Deepest lake in England

Wastwater differs from most of the more visited lakes in being the most remote and awe-inspiring. Many believe it to be Britain's most beautiful lake, and in 2007 a view of Wastwater was voted Britain's favourite.

Of the large lakes, Wastwater is the least visited. One commentator described the impression gained by visitors who only see Derwentwater, Ullswater and Windermere, and never seeing Wastwater as "jaundiced".

It is England's deepest lake, with a bed 79m (258 feet) below the lake surface, and below mean sea-level, having been gouged out by ice. On the south-eastern side is its most dramatic feature, the Wastwater Screes, Formed from weathered volcanic rocks from the crags above the lake, the screes start on the bed of the lake and rise up almost 2000 feet to the crags below Whin Rigg and Illgill Head.

Norse settlers came here in the 9th and 10th centuries, leaving behind what is claimed as Britain's smallest church, St Olaf's. It is suggested that the roof timbers may have come from Viking longboats.

Wasdale Head is the start for climbing many of the Lake District's big mountains, including Scafell Pike, Great Gable and Pillar. In addition there are passes to Borrowdale, Great Langdale and Eskdale.

There is a National Trust Campsite at Wasdale Head, and a youth hostel at the southern end of the lake.

Visit Cumbria has a very good web site with lots of information on Wasdale. www.visitcumbria.com

Looking up Wastwater towards Great Gable

ACKNOWLEDGEMENTS

Photography acknowledgements

Photography was by David and Rosemary Watson, except for the following photographs or images, which are used with permission.

John Peel	Pages 4, 28	Tullie House Museum
Fell Racing	Pages 8, 9	Tony Greenbank
Hound Trailing	Page 12	Margaret Baxter
"	Page 13	Dennis Peare
Wrestling	Page 23	Tony Greenbank
Rydal Mount	Page 29	www.cumbriaphoto.co.uk
Alfred Wainwright	Page 30	Wainwright Society
Bluebird	Pages 34, 35	Ruskin Museum, Coniston
Ullswater Steamboats	Page 52	www.cumbriaphoto.co.uk
Grasmere Sports	Page 60	Tony Greenbank
Lakeland	Page 66	Lakeland